for Audrey:
with pleasure
in meeting you!
love,
    allison

CORPORAL MUSE

Sibling Rivalry Press, LLC

PO Box 26147

Little Rock, AR 72221

info@siblingrivalrypress.com

www.siblingrivalrypress.com

ISBN: 978-1-943977-50-5

This title is housed permanently in the Rare Books and Special Collections Vault of the Library of Congress.

First Sibling Rivalry Press Edition, October 2018

CORPORAL MUSE

MUSE ALLISON E. JOSEPH

SIBLING RIVALRY PRESS
LITTLE ROCK, ARKANSAS
DISTURB / ENRAPTURE

CONTENTS

DICTIONARY

Accept that you may never know
bounty like mine anywhere else—
constellation of words coursing
down each of my exacting pages,
each word I explain special, none
furtive or disappearing.
Grant that I'm superior to you—
how could you not see how I eliminate
ignorance, enlighten this dull world
just as you breathe, as you sleep?
Kind friends, it will be another seven
lifetimes before you exhaust my contents,
my depths of denotation and connotation,
notes on derivations, full etymologies.
Oh, you know you want to be
profound like me, precise and
quite necessary like me,
righteous in rectitude, contemporary,
stylish. No other book you own can
teach you more, for I decode those
urgent holes of meaning in all other
virtuous texts and missives, illuminating
willfully elusive paragraphs, accurate as
x-rays, diligent, always ready for work.
You open me, and worlds begin to shift,
zealously, you'll covet all I can define.

TERRESTRIAL

Some seek the paranormal and the strange,
the messages that come from someplace far
beyond our average lives. They look for change
in ordinary skies, check out the stars
for clues from distant worlds, for signs of life
not engineered by human minds or hands.
Some live to search for otherworldly strife,
uninterested in what this earth demands,
so sure that something bigger must exist
beyond our meager reach, our shaky grasp,
a grander world we can't control with fists
or bombs, vast galaxies to make us gasp.
But I prefer the world that I can find
by rummaging the wreckage in my mind.

THE JOINING

You're a wind-up toy I never tire of,
big as my thumb and just as funny.
You're a cold lick of smooth sherbet,
sweeter than limeade; you're a palm
I slide lotion over, working moisture
into driest pores. You crack me open
with a gasp, a grin, a witch's cackle.
You smell like a thorn feels. Don
Johnson in his *Miami Vice* suits
and Italian loafers has nothing on you,
my man. You mutant, you scorpion,
you're so small I might lose you,
so wide I'm aching. I'm happy
you aren't leaving—if you did, I'd have
to bear your child. That dog won't
hunt. That quiet dog of reticence
won't brandish a shotgun, kill us all.
Your rivers dry me out, use me up,
toss me by the roadside, left for dead.
For you, I'd swallow swords, walk
red coals, not a bird girl but a woman
of many talents, swami in denim,
truthteller, soothsayer who will do
her best soft shoe to make you rise.
I'm here because God sends women
to stimulate the gross national product
by seducing overworked men, and you're
my first, my only, my most gracious victim.
Mañana, spoons will dance, you will
spin, and I will never stop admiring
the juncture where you trail off, I begin.

NEW BOOK TALKING

Discover me. Pick me up and touch me,
my spine, my shiny, fresh-from-the-shop
sheen. Don't fold me, burn me, trash me,
or sell me back for pennies when you know
you paid much more. Don't crease my pages,
smear my type, or smudge my cover
with greasy pizza stains. Don't dribble
on me, or get crumbs in my folds, or
sweat on me after guilt-induced exercise.
Don't leave me outside so that rain
can erode me, pages stuck together,
sodden as leaves. Don't tell me you've
seen prettier; don't tell me I strain your eyes.
I am profound and important, and therefore
must be in small print. Don't fall asleep
with me on your belly, flaps spread,
your mind too dull to translate
my words into pictures, pictures
into meaning. Resist tucking me
away when I get difficult. Don't
give me to anyone you don't love.

SUSANNA JONES, NOW 80, WEARS RED FOR THE LAST TIME

after Langston Hughes

For you, Langston, I will wear red
once more, walking proudly as the queen
you swore I was, face still a regal cameo.
No other men loved me like you did—
no exclamations to Jesus, no proclamations
by trumpet, silver or otherwise.

For you, Langston, I will step out in red
one last time, red dress over this, my only body,
now sad with lost chances and children,
red heels like spikes of fire, red lips—

ones that still sing of you, Langston,
your Harlem nights, your Sugar Hill streets,
your songs for dark girls like me
now grown to women who no longer
wear red because you aren't here
to let us know we still can.

IF I WERE A SONG

you'd listen to me again and again,
trying to learn every word of my lyric—
every *tra la la* and *ooh baby, baby,*
every wordless mumble and stutter.

You'd buy the sheet music to study me,
play me on the piano until your fed-up
neighbors bang on the wall, sick
of my chords. If I were a song,

you'd want me on the radio every day,
spinning me in heavy rotation, every
hour on the hour. I'd go *Billboard* Hot
100, then top 40, then top 10, then

all the way to number one, top
of the pops, the hit parade, most
requested song in America for
the eleventh week in a row.

You'd hear me even in your sleep,
sing me in the shower, hot sudsy water
down your back. You'd play me until
the player quit, tape snapped, batteries dead.

A PLEA TO THE GRAMMAR LADY

Split infinitives slap me hard, slice
thin red scratches across my cheeks.

Modifiers dangle from me, slipping
off into nonsense before I can pull

them back. Tense about tenses,
I try to pin down the future, to prop

up the past, to liberate the present
from a pallid state of being. Participial

phrases shatter beneath my pen, broken
like so many molecules, so many particles

of nothing. Give me the decoder ring,
the 3-D x-ray glasses, the book

of runes and symbols, and help
decipher these inscrutable rules,

this i-before-e-except-after-c legislation.
Help me to sing despite this crippled tongue,

these hunched fingers, this unruly mind.

YOU CAN'T ALWAYS GET

Give me Christmas every single day—big bright
presents, succulent roast ducklings, no bills
to pay until February. Give me days of no rain,
no bleary gray skies penetrating my sinuses
and my mood, no soggy soil making me sink
into mud, into leaf-rot and muck that spoils
my best pair of ass-kicking boots.

Give me drunkenness without hangovers,
ecstasy without hallucinations,
excitement without consequences—
no blood   no scars   no broken bones
or chipped teeth. Give me girdles with no seams.

Give me chocolate without calories,
fried chicken without fat, grease that doesn't
turn to lard on my hips, an extra family
on my thighs. Give me mirth in the midst

of pain, laughter so fierce my sides ache,
a fit of giggles in the middle of class
that spreads from one student to another
until we are all laughing, roaring, rolling
on the floor, clutching our stomachs in hilarity.

Give me that, just once, and I won't
ask for anything again—for anything
as cosmic, nothing as divine.

CORPORAL MUSE

Dressed in drab olive green fatigues,
bayonet in fist, beret on his bald head,
he wants to see your work—pages and pages
of it. He wants you broken and crying,
sniffling and curled in a small ball
on the edge of your bed as you scratch
out your most heartfelt desires with the one
stubby pencil he permits you,
wood splintering under your thumb.
Pushing you down into the mud of your self,
he dares you to muck through all that tragedy
you think uniquely yours, all that angst
that makes you special. He kicks
the bed frame, rattles the mattress,
yells *Attention!* whenever you use
a worn word, clichés so abominable
that he threatens to kick you from the service
if you get within two sentences of one.
AWOL doesn't sound so bad right now,
as his heavy stinking breath taints your skin,
your ears, your fingers aching from clutching
this broken yellow twig, its nub of an eraser gone.
Give me twenty, he yells, and you wonder
what—twenty paragraphs, twenty pages, twenty words?
Bayonet pointed at your head, he quips,
Now who's got writer's block, eh, private?
smirking as you stutter, shuffle papers.
So much for writing that's private,

done in secrecy for a cherubic muse
who beamed at every page you finished.
You've got this sergeant instead,
with his muscles of brass and his black
combat boots, his dog tag, his bark
that won't stop thundering in your head.
You show him all you have, pages
fluttering in your grip. And he tears them up,
snarls, *Do IT Over,* and you do,
afraid of a dishonorable discharge,
a dishonest paragraph, an unearned lie.

POET'S LOVE SPELL

I want to be your favorite line,
that poem that you hum at night,
slick words you faithfully recite.
I want to be your favorite line,

that poem that you hum all night—
deft syllables that swell your sleep,
one treasured page you fold and keep.
That poem that you hum all night,

apt syllables that swell your sleep,
smooth sounds that calm your troubled lungs,
a hymnal's worth of prayers sung,
apt syllables that swell your sleep,

smooth sounds that calm your troubled lungs,
and ease that sobbing in your brain,
a link from me to you, sleek chain,
smooth sounds that ease your troubled lungs,

and soothe that sobbing in your brain.
I want to be that sacred psalm
to heal your wounds, to act as balm,
and soothe that sobbing in your brain.

I want to be your favorite line,
that poem that you hum at night,
those words you carefully recite.
I want to be your favorite line.

CHANCES ARE: AN UPDATE

Chances are, the mortgage hasn't been paid.

Chances are, the spot your doctor found in your
        left breast will be bigger by the time
        you see the specialist he recommends.

Chances are, the boy who took your daughter out
        has a knife in his back pocket,
        another girl's skin under his nails.

Chances are, the flutter in your husband's chest
        that he shrugs off as nothing
        is actually something, half his capacity for speech
        gone by the time the ambulance arrives.

Chances are, the neighbor who grows
        the brightest roses you ever saw
        is watching when you shower and rinse
        your slopes and curves, flesh
        both hotter and softer in the steam.

Chances are, you'll never realize it,
> too distracted wondering whether
> you put a stamp on the envelope
> you mailed the mortgage check in,
> too worried wondering about that spot
> your doctor says is probably nothing,
> just like the flutter in your husband's chest
> that builds to a thrum whenever
> you talk about that boy you let
> take your daughter out—
> his mouth on her face,
> his hands on her wrists.

IN PRAISE OF BUGS

Who couldn't help but love your cross-dressing,
wise-cracking self, fruit crowning your head,
sarong around your non-existent hips, lips

pursed red and ripe for a juicy smack?
Street hustler, flim-flam bunny, weren't you
everyone's first drag queen? Able to tunnel

miles and miles underground, sitter
to babyfaced gangsters, you made everyone
look foolish—woodenheaded Elmer,

dopey hunter whose gun you tied in bows,
that neurotic duck who always thought
himself superior, though he never made

anyone laugh—that monster whose hair
you did—sticks of TNT for curlers.
Such an interesting monster, too,

you purred, right before you blew his
head off. You showed me so many
career paths—farm-wrecker, cowboy

thrasher, deviant from my own planet,
hare from round the block and who
knows where, carrot ninja, joker

jouster, sanest trickster this side
of Albuquerque. You taught me which
holes to pop out of, how to torment

my tormentors, how to ad-lib and
smack-talk, how to live the most
authentic life anyone could on a

Saturday morning. I'll forgive you
for falling for that girl bunny robot.
When the air is Disney-thick

and full of Smurfs, I'll adore
you forever. Anyone who loves you
knows life is what's up, and we

better live it loud and wild,
chomping down on everything
that doesn't bite us first.

YESTERDAY, WE ALL GREW DESPERATE

Yesterday, we all grew desperate, turned away from the
Messy fireball in the sky. Who could deny that yesterday

A man too old to speak lost track of how many
Times he'd wrung his hands, that a girl, fingers burning,
Bled to draw a boy's profile in beach sand glittery

From broken-necked bottles, and a baby, launched
From a window, learned the velocity of the word *father?*

Ugly, yes, and yesterday, we whispered these legends—
Kneeling in bathrooms, in hall closets,
In classrooms of abandoned schools—

Ancient desks carved as totem poles.
Yesterday, two lovers destined for each other

Boarded trains in opposite directions, never met;
Two sisters left their mother's grave, furious
And mute, bickering over her favorite flower.

Stroking his boss's thighs, a husband forgot
His wife's middle name. Pies melted under

Hot light, twirling on glass-cased pedestals
In a diner where every last patron's gone diabetic.
Yesterday, we all woke breathless, frightened

By how each cell shrunk during sleep, some
New bruise or snatch of wrinkles glaring
In sunlight's ruthless alarm. Yesterday,

A boy stroked a gun like a body, bullets
Socked into its chamber by the felon

Who slid it onto his palm because two
Folded twenties from a twelve-year-old
Can buy the power that stops the shaking.

We all grew desperate and hungry,
Fingers scratching cheeks and chalkboards,
Fists punching holes and chins.

Yesterday, under that broad yellow eye, we all
Grew untethered, unable to sit still or curl up,

Unable to speak except for screams
Dispatchers defused all across the cities' blistered
Facades, counties' shanties, suburbs' vicious cul-de-sacs.

MOURNING: AN ART

after Elizabeth Bishop

The art of mourning isn't hard; it's hell,
despite the funerals, the florid wreaths.
I had two friends; and I'm not doing well

without them here. Who can I stop to tell
about their lives, their words, their griefs?
The art of mourning isn't hard; it's hell

to know we will not speak again, not dwell
in presences that once brought me relief.
I had two friends and I'm not doing well

without their lines, their images to swell
my memory, their ground time here too brief.
The art of mourning isn't hard; it's hell

to write about them now, to think and spell
when sorrow's shaking all of my beliefs.
I had two friends and I'm not doing well

without their voices here to soothe and quell
my fears, still cursing death, that stealthy thief.
The art of mourning? It's too hard, this hell.
Come back, my friends. You know that I'm not well.

POEM ARGUING WITH A LINE FROM MILOSZ:

What reasonable man would like to be a city of demons?

Maybe no reasonable man,
but truly an unreasonable woman,
singing her kind of songs
on a rainy evening streetcorner
soaking wet while all the proper girls
go to the gym or cupcake shop.
Unreasonable women write poems
with cities of angels and demons
in their heads, syllables and synapses
lit while their laundry spins another
tedious cycle in the hotshot dryer,
socks losing their mates as they
dream. Unreasonable women
are haunting me as I write,
being an unreasonable woman
myself, barren and brittle
but still brimming, dried bouquet,
funeral wreath, secret agent
of misery and motion. I want
to be a whole country of demons,
a gang of archangels, a burden
of demi-gods and semi-heathens.
I want to be largely sane,
but mostly crazy, crazed
as a city full of possessed souls
must be, orphaned as they are
by a town of reasonable men.

SELF-PORTRAIT AS ICE CREAM TRUCK

Always welcome, I glide through your
neighborhood, one repeating tune
on an endless loop to seduce
the smallest and eldest out
of barricaded homes and into

the streets, crying as if the
Messiah's come. Loyal to all
my flavors—you cannot—do not—
resist me, knowing all it takes
is a pocketful of change

to the man inside me to get
what I have to give: frozen
sugar on a stick, chocolate
frosted into submission,
sandwiches you nibble and lick

as if you'll never be granted
another, glorious soft-serve
squeezed into spirals and curls.
I am here to make you lose
your minds, make you forget

your diet and your last name,
every cell in your timid body
ready to shove a six-year-old
should she dare cut in front.

Cold as they come, I got you
on lock, silver body stealthy
on these ordinary streets, sleek
machine full of rainbows and push-ups,
strawberry shortcake and bomb-pops.
Should you try to resist me,

if you stay silent while everyone
clamors for my sweet tastes,
I'll make sure my music
never leaves your brain,
endless loop stunning you from sleep.

IN PRAISE OF WUSSY BOYS

I love their tousled hair and sloppy clothes,
they way they bump into you, stammer your name,
then disappear before you can reply. I love them
miserable over guitar strings, trying to strum

something faint and beautiful before it's gone,
before she's gone and moved away, or left
for work, or left for some surly guy's he-man
love shack. I love them tall and slender or

short and round or non-descript and in-between;
I love them black, white, Asian, mixed, mottled,
Spanish-speaking, German-reading, balding,
hesitant-to-smile or grinning so broadly they

might trip over their own teeth. I like them
with lost buttons they're too clumsy to sew
back on, but love them most in the kitchen—pots
boiling, propped cookbooks threatening to fall

off the counter's edge, something ginger-spicy
and unidentifiable heating up the house. Wussy
boys don't cheat at Scrabble, don't lie to your
mother, don't pilfer checks from your account

without telling you. Wussy boys like all those
parts of a woman make-up can't fix: wrinkles
on a neck, scars on the back, stretch marks
on breasts, belly, thighs. A wussy boy is strong

enough to bring to a wedding or a funeral, strong
enough to survive a phalanx of sloshed uncles,
sober aunts. He doesn't read your notebooks
unless you tell him to, has no use for smut

but loves erotica, knows your middle name,
your mother's maiden name, your sister's allergies,
the shoe size you claim and the shoe size you wear.
Most of all, a wussy boy is just strong enough

to kiss you until you know they're more man
than boy, until you want what's beneath those sloppy
clothes more than you want breakfast, lunch,
and dinner, more than you want your dignity intact.

NIGHT WATCH FOR TRAVELING HUSBAND

Night feels thicker when you are gone,
heavier, full of deceptive shapes
and roaming cars that could be yours,

but aren't. I'm such a silly girl, waiting
for your return, cool patience of the long-
married replaced by bubbling anxiety,

shape-shifting tension unrelieved
by the madly barking dogs next door
who resume their frenzy anytime

any vehicle approaches. Should I
go to the window one more time,
peer through curtains one more time,

hoping you are off the highways
and at last onto local streets,
descending into neighborhoods

you know, coming around
the cul-de-sac, tires gliding
onto the driveway? Sleepless,

fretting, I know exactly how far
away you are, mark off miles on a
mind's eye map, know where

you will fill up or stop to eat,
but I still hope to see you
sooner than the speed limit allows,

damning any incident or accident
that clogs the interstate, any cop
with a quota to be made, any

construction site with vested
stop-sign workers. Night,
bring him back to me before

you tumble into day, before hated
sunrises and solo breakfasts.
Night, release him to my lair.

TO SYLVIA

Mistress of the miserable,
the tormented girl I was
loved you so, your madness

as mutable as the pages
I ripped from *Ariel*,
The Bell Jar, damaged books

unfit for the library—
my contraband, all your
sutured words hidden

under my bed, stashed
like candy, like teen
magazines. I liked

your father rage,
anger I could never
show to mine, your militant

stanzas honed and perfect
as your blond pageboy.
Somehow I thought

you knew me, though
I had no idea
what your madness

tasted like, that shock
of electricity crawling
your spine. You

made it okay to ache
at the fringes of feeling,
to be haunted by a future

that hadn't even started yet.
Even now, a line of yours thrills
as it slashes the thin skin

that keeps my sanity
intact, though you are
mentioned as some

errant punch line, some
talk show host's easy
joke. I know some

girl, some sad girl,
is opening a book
of your lines right now,

and she's feeling
the rigor of your exquisite pain,
pangs of your gassed heart.

NECESSITIES

I do not wait for God to learn to pray,
I do not wait for hope to learn those pleas.
No need for boundaries to set me free,
No need for games to hustle me to play.

My legs don't need the fearlessness to fail,
my heart no need for ache to feel each thrust
of pleasure or of pain. Each fingernail
will crack or peel or break, no need for lust

to color my dull fingertips. No need
to speak aloud the visions in my breath,
no need to share the headaches in my sight
that dazzle me to brilliant, sweaty depths.

Each syllable another life's pushed through—
I only need these words I pledge to you.

ACKNOWLEDGMENTS

Poems from this collection appeared in the following magazines:

"In Praise of Wussy Boys": *North American Review*

"Chances Are: An Update": *Cream City Review*

"Susanna Jones, Now 80, Wears Red for the Last Time": *Quercus Review*

"If I Were a Song": *Atlanta Review*

"Dictionary," "Enough": *Verseweavers* (Oregon Poetry Society)

"Self-Portrait as Ice Cream Truck": *Taos Journal of Poetry and Art*

"To Sylvia": *Fledgling Rag*

"Night Watch With Traveling Husband": *Whale Road Review*

ABOUT THE AUTHOR

Allison E. Joseph lives in Carbondale, Illinois, where she is Professor of English and Director of the MFA Program in Creative Writing at Southern Illinois University. She serves as editor and poetry editor of *Crab Orchard Review*. Her books and chapbooks include *What Keeps Us Here* (Ampersand Press), *Soul Train* (Carnegie Mellon University Press), *In Every Seam* (University of Pittsburgh Press), *Worldly Pleasures* (Word Tech Communications), *Imitation of Life* (Carnegie Mellon UP), *Voice: Poems* (Mayapple Press), *My Father's Kites* (Steel Toe Books), *Trace Particles* (Backbone Press), *Little Epiphanies* (NightBallet Press), *Mercurial* (Mayapple Press), *Mortal Rewards* (White Violet Press), *Multitudes* (Word Poetry), *The Purpose of Hands* (Glass Lyre Press), *Double Identity* (Singing Bone Press), and *What Once You Loved* (Barefoot Muse Press). Her most recent full-length collection, *Confessions of a Barefaced Woman*, was published by Red Hen Press in 2018. She is the literary partner and wife of poet and editor Jon Tribble.

ABOUT THE PRESS

Sibling Rivalry Press is an independent press based in Little Rock, Arkansas. It is a sponsored project of Fractured Atlas, a nonprofit arts service organization. Contributions to support the operations of Sibling Rivalry Press are tax-deductible to the extent permitted by law, and your donations will directly assist in the publication of work that disturbs and enraptures. To contribute to the publication of more books like this one, please visit our website and click *donate*.

Liz Ahl

Stephanie Anderson

Priscilla Atkins

John Bateman

Sally Bellerose & Cynthia Suopis

Jen Benka

Dustin Brookshire

Sarah Browning

Russell Bunge

Michelle Castleberry

Don Cellini

Philip F. Clark

Risa Denenberg

Alex Gildzen

J. Andrew Goodman

Sara Gregory

Karen Hayes

Wayne B. Johnson & Marcos L. Martínez

Jessica Manack

Alicia Mountain

Rob Jacques

Nahal Suzanne Jamir

Bill La Civita

Mollie Lacy

Anthony Lioi

Catherine Lundoff

Adrian M.

Ed Madden

Open Mouth Reading Series

Red Hen Press

Steven Reigns

Paul Romero

Erik Schuckers

Alana Smoot

Stillhouse Press

KMA Sullivan

Billie Swift

Tony Taylor

Hugh Tipping

Eric Tran

Ursus Americanus Press

Julie Marie Wade

Ray Warman & Dan Kiser

Anonymous (14)

CPSIA information can be obtained
at www.ICGtesting.com
Printed in the USA
BVHW032028110719
553242BV00001B/30/P